W9-AGH-017

Glass & Ceramic
PAINTING

KRISTEN JONES

MINI · WORKBOOK · SERIES

MEREHURST

CONTENTS

*Rooster mural (top), lotus flower vase (far left) and
kitchen canisters (left)*

You do not need to make a major investment to add colour and character to your home. This collection of tools and materials is about all you will need to get started, and the technique of painting on glass and ceramic is easy to learn.

Tools and materials

Painting on glass and ceramic is a very simple and effective way to update the look of a room, or to add a splash of colour to a tired corner. You do not need a lot of equipment to get started and the painted items can be fired in your domestic oven.

PAINTS

There are many types of paints suitable for painting on glass and ceramic, so check carefully with the manufacturer's instructions to ensure the paint you select is suitable for your purposes. Water-based glass and ceramic paints are formulated for use on glass and on glazed and fired ceramics, china and crockery. (Do not confuse these with greenware ceramics or the pottery that is made by throwing clay on a wheel—an entirely different type of paint and firing method is used for these.)

Generally, glass and ceramic paints are for decorative purposes and are not food-safe; that is, the painted area should not come into contact with your mouth, or with food or drink. This does not mean your creations can't be functional too: design them so the paint is on the outside of the glass or bowl, or leave the contact area unpainted.

The projects in this book use two types of paint: water-based glass and ceramic paints, and artists' acrylic paints. Both can be oven-fired, but they are used in different ways.

• Water-based glass and ceramic paints are suitable for use on china, crockery, terracotta and glass, and can be fired in a domestic oven to increase their durability.

Most ranges of glass and ceramic paints include an outliner paste. These are usually sold in tubes and are squeezed out through a fine tip to form a raised outline (useful for containing areas of paint and providing a strong outline for your design). For projects where a thicker paint coverage is required, outline paste can be used instead of paint.

Liquid leading performs a similar function to outliner paste, but the

---

SAFETY

Although glass and ceramic paints are non-toxic, they do not necessarily comply with food safety regulations. It is recommended that if the painted item will be in contact with food or drink, the areas that touch the food or the mouth should be left unpainted. Leave a gap for lips at the top of glasses and cups, and only paint the outside of bowls and jugs. Always read the manufacturer's instructions for the particular paint you are using.

HINT

Always carry out a few tests
before firing your finished piece,
particularly if you are painting
and firing a number of items at
once (e.g. a dinner set).

---

technique for using it is different (see
page 35). Unlike outliner paste,
liquid leading can not be fired.

You may also find a sealer, or filler
undercoat, is useful. If using
terracotta, always seal the porous
surface before use.

• Artists' acrylic paints can also
be used to paint on glass and ceramic
but they need to be mixed with a
glass and tile painting medium to
produce a paint suitable for firing.
This is a convenient alternative to
glass and ceramic paints as you may
already have an extensive range of
acrylic paints that can be used. The
general rule is to add three parts
medium to one part paint (3:1) and
mix thoroughly before painting, but
always check the manufacturer's
directions. The paints can then be
oven-fired to increase their durability.

See page 11 for general firing
instructions for both these paints.

BRUSHES
You only need a few brushes to get
started. Begin with the basics and
gradually build up your collection.
You will need:
• fine, round brushes
• larger, flat brushes
• stencil brushes

ETCHING CREAM
Etching creams can be purchased
from craft stores and there are several
brands available. The cream is
applied over a stencil or can be
painted directly onto glass or mirror.
Always follow the manufacturer's
instructions and wear rubber gloves.

SPONGES
Sponges are an invaluable decorating
tool. Their absorbent and uneven
surfaces produce wonderful textures.
A variety of types is available:
• Natural sea sponges are perfect for
applying a rough, textured paint
finish—try overlapping colours for a
mottled effect.
• Finer kitchen sponges give a more
even paint coverage and are useful
for detailed designs or for stencilling.
• Use roller sponges to apply a fine,
even coverage to an area.

RULERS
Use a plastic or metal ruler for
drawing up designs, but always use a
metal ruler when cutting stencils or
masks with a scalpel (the blade will
slice the edge of a plastic ruler). A
flexible tape measure is useful for
measuring circumferences.

SCISSORS AND SCALPEL
These are used to cut stencils or self-
adhesive vinyl (see page 7).
Regularly replace your scalpel blade
to ensure a neat, clean cut. Use a
scalpel to scrape off uneven paint
edges or errors (when the paint is
dry, but before it is fired).

COMPASS

A compass is used to draw accurate circles directly on the surface, or to create circular masks and stencils.

CUTTING MAT

This is essential for protecting your work surface when cutting stencils and masks. You can also use an old board or a wad of newspaper to protect the surface when cutting.

PENCILS

Soft pencils (2B or 4B) are useful for sketching out your design. Use a harder pencil (H) when transferring designs using carbon paper.

Use wax pencils to draw directly on to ceramics, glass and tiles, and to transfer designs onto surfaces without the need for tracing and carbon paper (see the box on page 10). This is the preferred method of transferring designs when you want to be able to see the pattern or surface underneath. Wax pencil marks wash off easily with warm, soapy water.

MASKING TAPE

Masking tape is used to mask off edges and areas which are not to be painted, or when you want to obtain a sharp, neat line, such as stripes. Use masking tape to hold stencils, tracing paper and patterns in position.

SELF-ADHESIVE VINYL

This is used for masking out areas that are to remain paint free when stencilling or sponging. Tinted or opaque adhesive vinyl is easier to see

---

HINT

Use a cotton bud to wipe off small mistakes. If the paint has dried and is difficult to remove, dip the cotton bud in a little hot water first and then carefully wipe off the paint.

---

than clear types when it is stuck onto white surfaces. It is available in sheets or rolls and can be cut to any shape and easily wrapped around curved surfaces. Self-adhesive dots (sold at most newsagents) make handy, small circular masks.

STENCIL CARDBOARD

This is a lightweight cardboard that is thin enough to cut easily with a scalpel, yet rigid enough to withstand several applications of paint.

TRACING MATERIALS

• Carbon/graphite paper is a sheet of paper with carbon on one side. It is placed between the pattern and the object to be painted (with the carbon side touching the surface of the object). The pattern is placed on top and a hard pencil is used to transfer the design onto the surface.

• Tracing paper (or greaseproof paper) is a sheet of transparent paper used to trace patterns.

PALETTE

A palette is useful for mixing paint colours and mediums. A plastic painter's palette, a tile, a saucer or an old ice cream lid can all be used.

Like any new skill, painting on glass and ceramics takes time and patience to master. For best results, always draw your design on paper first, then practise painting it a few times on an old tile or piece of glass.

Basic techniques

This book covers the different techniques for sponging, stencilling and painting on glass and ceramics, and for etching glass. Each project has step-by-step instructions for you to follow, but you may need to refer back to this chapter for more detail.

PREPARATION

1 Before you begin painting, ensure your glass or ceramic is completely free of dust and oil. Carefully clean the surface to be painted with a grease-cutting detergent in warm water. Remove all dust, fingerprints or smudges and rinse the detergent off thoroughly.

2 Allow the pieces to completely air-dry, or use a lint-free cloth.

SIZING THE DESIGN

3 The templates for the projects in this book are located on pages 55–62. Enlarge or reduce the pattern on a photocopier to achieve the desired size, or to the size indicated on the pattern. As most photocopiers only enlarge up to 200 per cent at a time, you may need to enlarge the design two or three times to get it to the correct size (if the design is large, tape pieces of A3 paper together).

Alternatively, use the grid method to enlarge the pattern (this is not recommended for detailed designs). Photocopy the pattern and draw a grid of squares over the design. On a separate piece of paper, draw a square or rectangle to the finished size and draw up another grid of squares (with the same number of squares as the original, but larger). Copy the design, square for square, onto the grid.

4 Place the enlarged design (either photocopied or enlarged using the grid method) over carbon paper, with the carbon side touching the surface to be painted, and fix both

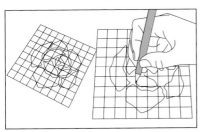

3 Draw a grid over the original design and copy the design, square for square, onto a larger grid.

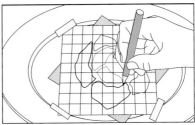

4 Place the design over carbon paper and fix both pieces of paper onto the surface with masking tape.

TRANSFERRING THE DESIGN

In addition to tracing outlines, there are a number of other ways that original designs can be transferred onto the surface to be painted (see step 5).
• When painting clear glass, stick the patterns behind the glass, or roll the pattern into a cone and place it in the glass.
• Draw the design directly on the surface to be painted using a wax pencil. The pencil marks can be wiped off with a cloth dampened in warm, soapy water.
• Trace the pattern onto a piece of tracing paper using a black pen. Turn the paper over and colour over the back of the tracing paper with a wax or soft pencil. Face the design right way up and tape the tracing paper to the surface to be painted. Trace over the design with a hard pencil to transfer the design on to the object.

Stick the pattern inside the glass so the design can be viewed from the front.

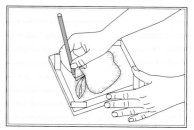

Rub the back of the design with a wax pencil, then trace over the outline with a hard pencil.

pieces of paper onto the surface with masking tape.

5 Transfer the pattern by tracing over the outline of the design with a hard pencil. See the box above for other methods of transferring designs.

PAINTING TECHNIQUES

6 Choose the size of brush to suit the area you want to paint. Before starting your project, practise your brush strokes (particularly fine lines) on scrap paper or a spare tile or glass.

7 To build up depth of colour, allow the first coat of paint to dry before adding the next. If you do not allow

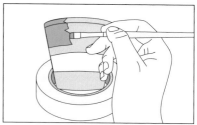

8 When painting glasses, jars or small pots, rest the objects inside a roll of tape to avoid holding them.

GENERAL OVEN-FIRING INSTRUCTIONS

Only paint and fire oven-safe glassware, ceramics and tiles. If you are unsure of the strength of your piece, test fire it before painting. Allow the paint to dry for at least 24 hours before firing.

• If using glass and ceramic paint:
Place your painted item in a cold oven and set the temperature to 150–160 degrees Celsius. Bake for 35 minutes, timing from when the temperature stabilizes at the desired level. Turn the oven off and allow the item to cool before opening the door. Hot glassware and ceramics are fragile and can crack if exposed to sudden changes in temperature.

• If using acrylic paint mixed with tile painting medium:
Place the painted item in a cold oven. Set the oven temperature to 165 degrees Celsius. Maintain this temperature for 30–45 minutes; turn the oven off and leave the item to cool before removing it.

OVEN-FIRING

9 Allow the paint to air-dry for at least 24 hours before firing it in the oven (thicker applications of paint may take longer to dry). This sets the paint, making it more durable. If the paint is not dry, it may bubble.

10 Respect the manufacturer's recommended oven temperatures and times, and use an oven thermometer to check the temperature.
• If times and oven temperatures are reduced, glazing may not occur.
• If oven temperature and firing times are increased, colours tend to brown, although hardness will improve.
• For larger items, oven times should be extended by about 5–10 minutes.
• Be aware that some paint colours darken on baking.

See the box on the left for general oven-firing times and techniques.

11 Once the item has reached room temperature, remove it from the oven, but handle it with care as the paint will be tender for several hours.

CARE OF FINISHED ITEMS

12 Once oven-fired, the painted piece can be washed using a cloth dipped in tepid, soapy water, but do not soak it. Never wash painted glass or ceramics in a dishwasher.

If the piece you are painting is fragile and is intended for decorative purposes only, you may not need to fire it. If this is the case, never wash the piece; only dust or wipe it gently to clean it.

the paint to dry thoroughly, it may become lumpy. To stop your work looking patchy, always use brushstrokes in the same direction.

8 When painting round items such as glasses, jars or small pots, rest the objects inside a roll of tape. By stabilizing the items in this way, your hands are kept free for painting.

This jug and plate set is for decorative purposes only. Do not sponge the paint near the rim of the jug or in the centre of the plate if you intend to use them to serve food and drink.

Sponged milk jug and plate

The irregular surface of a sea sponge creates a lovely textured pattern on these ceramic items. The secret to success is to use the paint sparingly and build up the depth of colour. Always practise sponging on paper before you commit to your ceramic pieces.

METHOD

1 Mask off the inside rim of the plate using masking tape.

2 Smear a small amount of dark blue paint over a plate or palette: you do not want the paint to be too thick or the holes in the sponge will clog up with paint. Dip the sponge into the

EQUIPMENT

- White ceramic plate
- White ceramic milk jug
- Masking tape
- Water-based glass and ceramic paint: dark blue
- Palette
- Large sea sponge
- Cotton buds

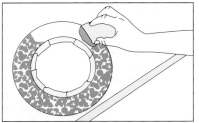

2 Dip the sea sponge in the blue paint and lightly sponge around the rim of the plate.

paint and dab off the excess paint onto a piece of scrap paper. Lightly sponge around the rim of the plate, turning the sponge as you work to avoid a repetition of the pattern. Frequently dip the sponge in the paint to achieve an even paint coverage. When the paint is dry, you may want to apply a second light coat. Remove the masking tape.

3 Use a damp cotton bud to wipe off any paint that may have leaked underneath the tape.

4 Sponge the outside of the milk jug (including the area under the handle) using the same technique as for the plate. As this jug is for decorative purposes only, the lip of the jug can also be sponged. Clean up any paint errors with a cotton bud. Wash the paint out of the sponge using warm, soapy water.

5 Allow the plate and the jug to dry for 24–48 hours. Place the items in a cold oven. Set the oven temperature to 150–160 degrees Celsius and bake for 35 minutes. Turn off the oven and allow it to cool before removing the plate and jug from the oven.

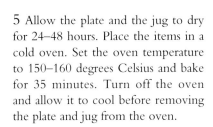

Terracotta pots

These charming pots are an ideal project for beginners. Blue ceramic paint is mixed with cream to achieve different shades of colour. The colours take on full depth and vividness after firing.

METHOD

1 Mask the three pots about halfway down the side with masking tape. Press the tape down firmly to prevent paint leakage under the tape.

2 Using the flat brush, thoroughly coat the top half of the pot, the rim and the inside with filler undercoat. This seals the porous surface of the pots and gives a stronger paint coverage. Repeat this process for the other two pots. Follow the manufacturer's guidelines for drying.

3 Paint the top half of the first pot with cream. Paint the lip of the pot and 2 cm down the inside of the pot as well. To paint the light blue pot, mix cream and blue in a ratio of 4:1 (4 parts cream and 1 part blue). Paint the blue pot with a mixture of cream and blue in a ratio of 1:1. The pots may need two to three coats for maximum opaqueness. Allow the paint to completely dry between coats. Remove the masking tape.

4 Leave the pots to dry for at least 48 hours before firing them in the oven. Place them in a cold oven on a stable surface. Set the temperature to 150–160 degrees Celsius and bake for 35 minutes. Turn off the oven and allow it to cool completely before removing the pots.

EQUIPMENT

- Three small terracotta pots
- Masking tape
- Paint brush: no. 6 flat
- Undercoat or sealer, suitable for terracotta
- Water-based glass and ceramic paints: cream, dark blue
- Palette

HINT

Always remove the masking tape (or self-adhesive vinyl) while the paint is still slightly wet. This will prevent the glue from lifting any dried areas of paint.

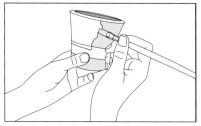

3 Using the flat brush, paint the top half of the first pot with cream. Paint over the rim and inside the pot.

Glass and ceramic paints work just as well on terracotta, but you do need to seal the terracotta first to ensure a solid coverage of paint. These little pots look best when displayed as a group of three or more.

Choose a plate with a wide rim so the design will fit neatly and comfortably around the edge. When buying the plate, it may be a good idea to take the design with you. Alternatively, reduce the size of the fish to suit your plate.

Decorative plate

Although this fish does have some areas of detail, you do not need advanced painting skills to achieve results such as this. A combination of masking and sponging techniques is used to complete the main body of the fish. Then, it is only a matter of adding in the black details by hand.

EQUIPMENT

- Pencil
- Self-adhesive vinyl (see page 7)
- Masking tape
- Scalpel
- Cutting mat
- Large, white china plate
- Tape measure
- Compass
- Small, self-adhesive dots
- Water-based glass and ceramic paints: light blue, dark blue, yellow, black
- Palette
- Sea sponge
- Cotton buds
- Round paint brushes

PREPARATION

1 Using a photocopier or the grid method, enlarge the design for the fish as indicated (the pattern is on page 56). Photocopy four fish at the correct size and tape them over a sheet of self-adhesive vinyl. Cut out the paper and vinyl together, using the scalpel and cutting mat.

2 Use a tape measure to find the centre of the plate and mark it with a pencil. Place a compass on this point and set it to fit the radius of the inner part of the plate (see Hint, page 18).

3 Using the compass, draw a circle on the sheet of self-adhesive vinyl. Cut out the circle using the scalpel and stick the vinyl down in the

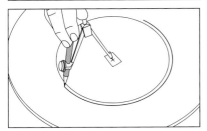

2 Place a compass on the centre of the plate and set it to fit the diameter of the inner part of the plate.

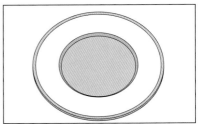

3 Mask off the centre of the plate using a circle cut from self-adhesive vinyl. Mask off the rim as well.

HINT

When using a compass to draw circles on a ceramic plate, to stop the compass slipping place a piece of masking tape in the centre of the plate.

centre of the plate. (This may be easier if you remain in one position and rotate the self-adhesive vinyl, thus maintaining a fluid movement and producing a neater cut.) Mask the outer rim of the plate with masking tape or strips of vinyl.

4 Position the four fish on the plate, spacing them at equal distances around the rim. Stick the self-adhesive dots randomly around the rim to fill in the spaces between the fish. Smooth all the masks down to remove any air bubbles and to ensure they are stuck firmly on the plate to prevent the paint from seeping in under the edges.

PAINTING THE DESIGN

5 Pour a small amount of light blue paint on the palette. Dip the sponge in the paint, dab off the excess and sponge a light layer of paint around the rim. While the paint is still wet, sponge a layer of dark blue paint over the top. If the paint is still wet, the colours will blend together nicely.

6 Remove the vinyl, small dots and masking tape while the paint is still wet. Clean up any smudged areas with a damp cotton bud.

7 Using the no. 3 round brush, paint in the fish shapes with yellow. You may need two or three coats to achieve a solid coverage.

8 Using the no. 3 brush and yellow, paint evenly spaced stripes (or small dabs of paint) around the outer rim. Leave to dry for at least 24 hours.

9 Using a small round brush and black paint, add in the details on the fish. Follow the photograph on the right as a guide. Do not worry if you make a mistake—because the yellow paint has been allowed to dry overnight, it can be carefully wiped clean of any unwanted paint with a

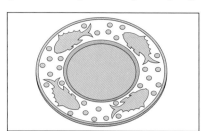

4 Position the fish masks on the plate, placing them equally apart. Place the dots randomly around the rim.

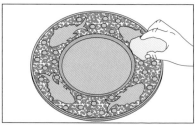

5 Sponge a layer of light blue around the rim, and then sponge a layer of dark blue over the top.

Add in the details on the fish using black and the fine brush.

cotton bud. However, do be gentle when wiping the design because although the paint is dry, it has not been fired and it is not that strong.

10 Allow the plate to dry for about 24–48 hours before firing. Put the plate in a cold oven and set the oven temperature to 150–160 degrees Celsius and bake for 35 minutes. Turn off the oven and allow the temperature to cool completely before removing the plate.

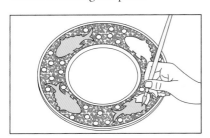

7 Fill in the fish using yellow. You may need a few coats to achieve a solid coverage.

CARE OF BRUSHES AND SPONGES

Brushes and sponges last for much longer if they are cleaned properly as soon as you have finished using them. For water-based paints, use water and household detergent.

1 Rinse the brushes in running water to remove the excess paint.

2 Rub the detergent into the brush, working it into the bristles. Rinse well with water. Squeeze out the water and shape the bristles with your fingers.

3 Allow the brushes to dry flat by placing them over the edge of the table: never stand them (or leave them to soak) in a jar brush downwards as this will bend the bristles out of shape.

4 Clean sponges in warm, soapy water. Rinse well to remove any soapy residue.

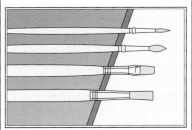

3 Shape the bristles with your fingers and leave them to dry on the edge of a table.

Kitchen canisters

Decorate ceramic kitchenware to match your other kitchen accessories or colour scheme. These canisters were purchased from a discount china shop and given a new lease of life by adding sponged stripes.

METHOD

1 Wash the canisters and lids thoroughly in warm, soapy water and allow them to air-dry. Remove any rubber seals from inside the lids.

2 Cut strips of masking tape and position them around the canisters to make masks for the stripes. Do not stick the tape down firmly until you are happy that the stripes are fairly even in width. These canisters have eighteen stripes; nine white and nine green (see Hand-painting stripes, page 25).

3 Dip the sea sponge in the paint and dab off the excess paint onto scrap paper. Lightly sponge over the exposed stripes. Allow to dry and apply a second coat. Remove the tape and leave to dry. Clean off any unwanted paint by gently scraping the surface with the edge of the scalpel blade.

4 Sponge the avocado paint roughly over the lids of the canisters, applying two coats to achieve the same depth of colour as the stripes. You may need to paint under the knobs with a paint brush to ensure coverage.

5 Allow the paint to dry for about 24–48 hours. Place the canisters and lids in a cold oven. Set the oven to 150–160 degrees Celsius and bake for 35 minutes. Turn off the oven and leave the items to cool before removing them. Once fully cooled, replace the rubber seals.

EQUIPMENT

- Three white ceramic oven-safe canisters
- Masking tape
- Sea sponge
- Water-based glass and ceramic paint: avocado
- Palette
- Scalpel
- Paint brush: no. 4 flat

3 Remove the masking tape and use a scalpel to scrape off any paint that may have leaked under the tape.

Masking tape is used to mask off the white stripes around the canisters. The width of the coloured stripe is slightly thinner than the masking tape.

The key to this project lies in the careful positioning of the fruit shapes. Avoid placing the pieces so that they all face the same way, instead angle them in different directions to make the design appear more natural.

Citrus bowl

This colourful design features four types of citrus fruit painted against a blue sponged background. The fruit pieces are painted using acrylic paints to which a glass and tile painting medium is added. Alternatively, use glass and ceramic paints.

EQUIPMENT

- Pencil
- Masking tape
- Self-adhesive vinyl
- Scalpel or scissors
- Cutting mat
- White ceramic bowl
- Water-based glass and ceramic paint: light blue
- Palette
- Large sea sponge
- Acrylic paints★: light yellow, red, ultramarine blue, brown earth, black
- Glass and tile painting medium★
- Paint brushes: no. 4 flat, no. 3 round
- Cotton buds

★ If preferred, substitute acrylic paints and the glass and tile medium for water-based glass and ceramic paints.

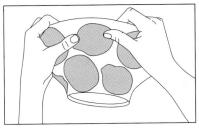

3 Lightly position the fruit masks around the bowl, adjusting their positions so they are evenly spaced.

METHOD

1 Using a photocopier or the grid method, enlarge the patterns for the fruit to the size indicated (see page 55). Tape the patterns onto a sheet of self-adhesive vinyl. Note that the same design is used for the orange and grapefruit (painted different colours), and the second design is used for the lemon and lime.

2 Using the scalpel, cut out enough masks to fit around the bowl. Alternatively, use a pair of scissors. Keep the shapes a little rough to add interest to the design. This bowl has sixteen motifs placed randomly around the outside of the bowl (four of each of the oranges, grapefruit, lemons and limes).

3 Peel off the adhesive backing from the vinyl and lightly position the masks around the bowl, maintaining an even amount of space between all the motifs. Try to alternate between lemons, limes, grapefruit and oranges. This may take a few attempts until you reach a pattern that is visually pleasing. Once this is done, firmly rub down all the vinyl masks to eliminate air bubbles and to prevent

Use watery brown to add shading and black dots to add texture to the fruit.

HINT

When painting the bowl, turn it upside down on the table. This will give you a more convenient angle to paint on.

the vinyl and masking tape while the paint is still slightly wet.

PAINTING THE FRUIT

5 The pieces of fruit are painted with acrylic paints mixed with a medium that makes them suitable for use on ceramics. Mix light yellow and red in a ratio of 2:1 (2 parts yellow to 1 part red). Then, mix the tile medium with the paint in a ratio of 3:1 (3 parts medium to 1 part paint). Using the flat brush, block in the oranges, leaving a small gap of white ceramic showing. Leave to dry before applying a second coat.

paint from leaking under the edges. Mask off an edge on the rim of the bowl with masking tape (the paint should not come in contact with food but, to be sure, always wash the fruit before eating it).

4 Put some light blue ceramic paint in the centre of the palette and dip the sponge in the paint. Dab off the excess paint on a piece of scrap paper and sponge an even background of blue around the fruit masks. Remove

6 Following step 5, block in the limes using ultramarine blue and light yellow mixed in a ratio of 1:4. Mix the glass and tile medium with the paint in a ratio of 3:1. Allow to dry and apply a second coat.

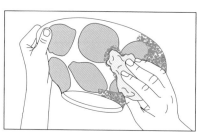

4 Using the sea sponge and blue paint, sponge over the background to build up an even tone of blue.

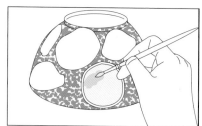

5 Mix light yellow and red to create a light orange colour and fill in the orange shapes.

7 Block in the lemons and grapefruit using light yellow and red mixed in a ratio of 3:1. Mix the glass and tile medium with the paint in a ratio of 3:1. Apply a second coat.

8 Once the fruit shapes are dry, add some shading around the edges of the fruit using a small amount of brown earth acrylic watered down with 5 parts of glass and tile painting medium. Leave to dry. Use black (mixed with tile medium) and the no. 3 round brush to add some small dots over the skin of the fruit.

9 Allow to dry for at least 24 hours. Place the bowl in a cold oven; set the temperature to 150–160 degrees Celsius and bake for 35 minutes. Turn off the oven and leave it to cool before removing the bowl.

HAND-PAINTING STRIPES

Often, the most difficult part of hand-painting stripes is achieving accurate spacing between the lines. This simple technique is useful when painting stripes that are all equal in width.

1 Wrap a piece of string around the circumference of the object and cut it to size.

2 Let's say the measurement is 30 cm (12 in). If you decide to make the stripes 2.5 cm (1 in) in width, then divide this number into 30 cm (12 in). This will give twelve stripes (you must always have an even number of stripes or you will end up with two of the same coloured stripes together).

3 Stick the string on a ruler and mark off twelve measurements, each of 2.5 cm (1 in) apart.

4 Wrap the string around the object and hold it in place with masking tape. Transfer the marks on the string around the circumference of the object.

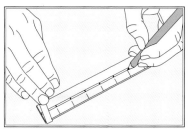

3 Stick the string on a ruler and use a pen to mark off points along the string, 2.5 cm (1 in) apart.

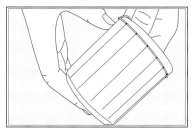

4 Transfer the marks onto the object to give you the width of the stripes. Draw out the stripes.

Glasses

This cheery floral design is perfect for sprucing up a set of plain drinking glasses. If you do not feel confident enough to paint the design in freehand, photocopy the pattern and stick it inside the glass so that you can trace over the design.

METHOD

1 Thoroughly clean the glasses and allow them to air-dry.

2 Photocopy the flower motif six times using the pattern on page 58. Cut out the images into small squares.

3 Stick a strip of masking tape around the glass so that the bottom edge of the tape measures 2.5 cm (1 in) from the top of the glass. Stick another piece of tape around the glass so that the top edge measures 5 cm (2 in) from the top of the glass. The band of glass visible between the tape is the area to be painted.

4 Using tape, fix the six patterns around the inside of the glass, positioning them so they are centred in the middle of the glass band. Space them evenly around the glass.

5 Load the round brush with burgundy paint. Following the pattern visible through the glass, press the entire head of the brush down on the glass to form a petal. Repeat for all six petals, adding a dot in the centre. Allow to dry and then repeat with a second coat, if necessary.

EQUIPMENT

- Three plain glasses
- Scissors
- Masking tape
- Ruler
- Paint brush: round no. 3
- Water-based glass and ceramic paints: burgundy, purple, light purple

Remove the tape and patterns. Repeat in purple and light purple for the other glasses.

6 Leave to dry for 24 hours before firing. Place the glasses in a cold oven (sit them on a ceramic tile if they are unsteady). Set the oven to 150–160 degrees Celsius and bake them for 35 minutes. Allow the glasses to cool in the oven before removing them.

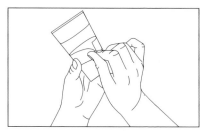

3 Wrap two pieces of masking tape around the glass to leave a band of glass visible.

When planning the design for your set of glasses, keep in mind that the painted area should be placed well below the rim. This will ensure that the paint does not come into contact with your mouth.

These tiles were painted and oven-fired before they were stuck on the wall. You can also decorate an existing white tiled wall in this manner, but remember that non-fired tiles are less resistant to scratching and splashing.

Kitchen tiles

Hand-painted tiles are expensive so a useful alternative is to decorate your own. Plain white tiles were used here—half of the tiles were decorated with a pretty pear stencil, and the other half were sponged using burgundy paint. The pear design is achieved using a three-part stencil: the pear, the leaves and the stems.

PREPARATION

1 Calculate how many tiles you will need. You may only want to add a row of tiles along the top of an existing tiled wall, or you may want to tile a large area behind a kitchen sink or bench. When you have decided this, divide the tiles into two groups. The first half will be decorated with the pear stencil and the second half will be sponged with burgundy.

You can also paint on tiles that are already positioned, but be aware that the awkward angle may make this a little difficult and tiring. Also, you will be unable to fire the tiles when the painting is completed.

2 Cut out three squares of cardboard the same size as your tiles.

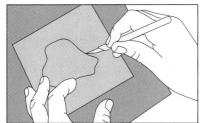

4 Transfer the pear shape onto the first piece of cardboard and cut out the shape with a scalpel.

3 Trace over the pattern for the pear using a piece of tracing paper (the pattern is on page 56). If you are using bigger tiles enlarge the design as needed.

4 Using carbon paper and a pencil, transfer the outline for the pear only onto one square of cardboard. Place the cardboard on a cutting mat and cut out the pear shape with a scalpel.

EQUIPMENT

- White ceramic tiles: 10 x 10 cm (4 x 4 in)
- Scissors
- Stencil cardboard
- Pencil
- Tracing paper
- Carbon paper
- Cutting mat
- Scalpel
- Masking tape
- Fine kitchen sponge
- Water-based glass and ceramic paints: mustard, dark green, light brown, burgundy
- Palette
- Tile adhesive and grout

Build up the shading on the pear using green in the centre and brown around the edges.

HINT

Do not worry if you make a mistake when stencilling the design: simply wash the paint off with warm, soapy water. Ensure the tile is completely dry before you use it again.

---

5 Following step 4, transfer and cut out the pattern for the leaves only, using the second piece of cardboard. Similarly, transfer and cut out the pattern for the pear stem and branch using the third piece of cardboard.

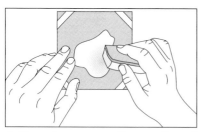

6 Tape the pear stencil to a tile and lightly sponge mustard paint over the exposed area of the stencil.

SPONGING THE DESIGN

6 Tape the stencil for the pear to a tile. Use the kitchen sponge to lightly sponge a layer of mustard paint over the exposed area. Start by dipping the edge of the sponge in the paint and then dab off the excess paint onto scrap paper. Build up the colour gradually—it is easier to add the colour slowly than to remove the paint if you have applied too much. Using dark green, lightly sponge over the centre of the pear to add highlights. Use light brown to shade around the bottom and side of the pear. Complete the basic pear shape for half of the tiles. Leave to dry.

7 Tape the stencil for the leaves over a dry pear tile, carefully aligning the piece of cardboard with the edges of the tile so that the patterns will match up correctly. Using dark green paint, sponge one or two layers to fill in the leaves. Repeat this process to add the leaves to all the pear tiles. Allow the paint to dry.

8 Tape the stencil for the stem and branch over a dry pear and leaf tile.

7 Tape the leaves stencil over a dry pear tile, and sponge in the leaves using dark green paint.

SPONGING

• You may find it easier to cut your kitchen sponge into smaller pieces. This makes it easier to handle, especially when sponging small areas.

• A kitchen sponge gives a much softer texture than a sea sponge and is the better option when sponging a detailed design.

Sponge one or two layers of light brown over the stencil. Repeat this process to complete all the pear tiles.

9 Pour a large amount of burgundy paint on the palette. Dip the sponge in the paint, dab off the excess onto scrap paper and sponge over the surface of the remaining tiles. Allow to dry before sponging a second and, possibly, a third layer. You want to achieve a fairly full coverage of paint.

10 Allow the tiles to dry for at least 48 hours and then fire them in the oven. Remember to do a test run by baking one or two tiles before you fire your whole set. Place the tiles in a cold oven. Set the oven temperature to 150–160 degrees Celsius and bake for 35 minutes. Turn off the oven and allow it to cool completely before removing the tiles from the oven.

11 Fix the tiles in place using a suitable adhesive (ask at your local hardware store to ensure a suitable choice). If preferred, grout between the tiles to finish.

HINTS

When using glass and ceramic paint or acrylic paint that has been mixed with a tile painting medium, take note of the following points.

• Some colours are quite transparent when first applied to the glass or ceramic. You may need to apply several layers if you want an opaque finish, but ensure you allow the paint to dry between coats. If the second coat is added too soon, the paint may become lumpy.

• When oven-firing your glass and ceramics, take care with oven temperatures and timing. If the oven is too hot, some paint colours may scorch and brown. If the oven is too cool, or firing time is too short, the paint will not harden sufficiently.

• It is recommended that you use an oven thermometer to check your oven's temperature.

• Do not bake the paints in a microwave oven.

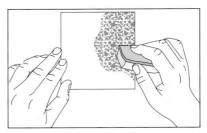

9 Dip the sponge into the burgundy paint, dab off the excess and sponge over the tile.

Here, the paint on the cabinet door was left to dry for several days. Then the timber was painted with a light coat of walnut stain mixed with Danish oil.

Faux stained-glass cabinet

Create the appearance of stained glass by using ordinary glass paints to transform a plain pine cabinet into a work of art. The leading used on the cabinet is actually purchased in a liquid form and squeezed out of a bottle to form strips. When dry, the leading strips can be bent to fit the contours of the design.

APPLYING THE LEADING

1 Using a photocopier, enlarge the pattern for the glass door to the size indicated, or as required (see page 57). To estimate how much leading you need to complete the project, use a tape measure and calculate the length of linework on the design. This cabinet uses about 10 metres (33 ft) of leading. It is always better to add 20 per cent extra to the estimated amount, to allow for any mistakes.

2 Tape the sheet of plastic to a flat surface. (If using a shopping bag, select one without any writing or printed patterns on it: the print may stick to the leading and the leading will not properly adhere to the glass.) Using the bottle of liquid leading,

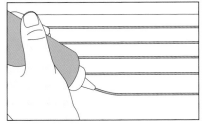

2 Using the bottle of liquid leading, squeeze a series of straight lines onto a thick sheet of plastic.

EQUIPMENT

- Tape measure
- Stencil plastic, heavy plastic sheet or shopping bag (see step 2)
- Liquid leading (see box on page 35)
- Scalpel
- Cutting mat
- Wooden cabinet with glass door
- Masking tape
- Paint brushes: no. 4 flat, no. 2 round
- Water-based glass and ceramic paints: purple, yellow, burgundy
- Palette
- Toothpicks
- Cotton buds

squeeze a series of straight lines on the plastic. Keep the tip of the bottle a small distance from the plastic surface and hold the tube at a slight angle. This will help to keep the thickness of the lines consistent and even. Produce enough lines to complete the design. Practise this a little until you are able to control the flow of leading from the bottle.

3 Allow the leading to dry for about three days. When dry, use a scalpel to

HINT

Some glass paints are sold in tubes
so you may be able to squeeze the
paint directly onto the glass
(within the confines of the
leading strips). You may still need
a brush or toothpick to spread the
paint out evenly.

*Flood the paint into the different
sections of the design. The leading acts
as a barrier and contains the paint.*

trim the ends off each strip and tidy
up any other irregularities.

4 Wash the glass on the cabinet door
with warm, soapy water to ensure it
is free of any grease or dust. Use a
clean, slightly damp cloth to rinse the
detergent off. Allow the glass to air-
dry or dry it with a lint-free cloth.

5 Lay the cabinet down flat with the
door facing upwards and tape the
pattern to the inside of the cabinet
door with masking tape. Ensure the
pattern is straight and centred within
the glass panel.

6 Carefully peel the lead strips off
the sheet of plastic and press them
onto the front of the glass using the

pattern as a guide for the leading to
follow. The lead will stick to the
glass as you press it down. Do not
overlap the strips, but use a scalpel to
trim the ends so the lines butt up
against each other. Do not throw the
small pieces away: they may be
needed to patch up areas later.

7 Fill in any gaps and joins with a
dab of the liquid leading. Leave the
leading to dry.

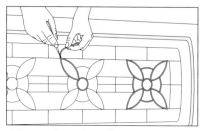

*6 Press the strips of leading onto the
glass following the pattern, and cut
the ends with a scalpel.*

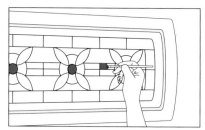

*9 Using the flat brush, dip the
bristles into the paint and drop the
paint into each segment.*

PAINTING THE GLASS

8 If preferred, remove the pattern from behind the glass so you have a better idea of the depth of colour when you are painting the glass.

9 Using the flat brush, dip the bristles in the paint and drop the paint into each segment, following the main photograph as a guide for colour. Drop in an ample amount of paint and spread it out with the brush. Make sure your leading lines are neatly butted together and firmly pressed onto the glass surface or the paint will leak into the next area. Add more paint to achieve a fairly even coverage that is not streaky. Use the smaller round brush to push the paint into the corners.

10 After you have applied the paint to one section, check for air bubbles and burst them with a toothpick.

11 Clean away smudges with a cotton bud and carefully scrape off any mistakes with the scalpel.

12 Allow the cabinet to dry flat for several days before turning it upright. If it is stood upright too early, the paint may pool at the bottom of each leaded section.

13 As the paint has not been oven-fired, treat it with care. The paint is quite durable but it will not stand up to harsh abrasives and constant wiping. Keep it clean with a soft cloth or a duster.

LIQUID LEADING OR OUTLINER PASTE?

When you want to create a raised outline for your design or imitate the leading used in stained glass, there are two products often used.

• Liquid leading (used for the cabinet, and the door, page 48) is usually purchased in a bottle or large tube, and is found in major craft stores. The liquid is squeezed out of the tube through a nib to form thin lines. When dry (after two or three days) it is hard but flexible enough to be bent and shaped as desired. No glue is needed to stick the leading strips to the glass: just press it on with your hands.

There are a few brands of liquid leading on the market, so ensure the product you select is suitable for your purposes. Always read the manufacturer's directions carefully and, if in doubt, check with the distributor. Liquid leading can be purchased from art and craft stores.

• Outliner paste (used for the window, page 46) is sold in a small tube and is found alongside most brands of glass and ceramic paints. The paste is squeezed out through a fine tip directly onto the surface to be painted. The outline is finer than liquid leading and the effect is not as authentic, but it is easier and cheaper to use. As with glass and ceramic paint, the outliner paste can be fired in the oven.

Lotus flower vase

Transform a plain glass vase with this simple but classic design, inspired by the lotus flower. The design is achieved by sponging black paint through a stencil made from self-adhesive vinyl.

METHOD

1 Using a photocopier, enlarge the pattern for the flower (located on page 60) to the size indicated, or to fit the vase. Tape the pattern onto a small piece of self-adhesive vinyl to use as a cutting guide.

EQUIPMENT

- Square glass vase
- Masking tape
- Self-adhesive vinyl
- Cutting mat
- Scalpel
- Water-based glass and ceramic paint: black
- Palette
- Small sea sponge
- Paint brush: no. 1 round
- Cotton buds

2 Using a scalpel and cutting mat, cut around the outer shape of the flower. Cut out the six inner parts of the flower (the white areas inside the petals). Set them aside.

3 Peel off the backing and stick the vinyl on the vase. Smooth it down to remove any air bubbles. Stick down the inner parts of the flower. Try to keep the negative spaces equal.

4 Using the sponge, apply the black paint thickly over the design. If necessary, sponge on a second layer. Carefully peel off the vinyl while the paint is still slightly wet.

5 Fill in any gaps using a paint brush and black paint. Allow to dry for at least 24 hours and then bake the vase in the oven (see page 11).

The lotus flower design.

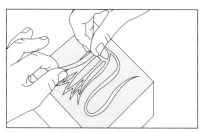

3 Place the design cut from self-adhesive vinyl on the vase. Then stick down the inner parts of the flower.

To ensure this elegant design looks its best, it is important to check that the vase receives a solid and even coverage of paint. This can be checked by holding the vase up to the light: you'll easily spot any patchy or thin areas of paint.

Choose a mirror for your project and then lay out the tiles around it to see how many you will need (you may need to cut the tiles so that they form a neat border). The mirror and the fired tiles are then glued onto a board.

Tiled mirror

Create a decorative tiled border for a mirror and add a touch of class to the hallway, bedroom or bathroom. This design uses a combination of sponging and easy hand-painting techniques.

METHOD

1 Enlarge the patterns for the long and corner tiles to the size indicated (see page 58). Stick the two patterns on two pieces of cardboard. Using a scalpel, cut out the floral shapes and the straight borders (not the swirls). Use a ruler to keep the lines straight.

2 Tape the long stencil on a long tile. Sponge two light layers of purple on the tile and leave to dry. To neaten the edges, fill in over the purple using the round brush loaded with red.

EQUIPMENT

• Cardboard
• Masking tape
• Scalpel
• Cutting mat
• Metal ruler
• White tiles: eight 60 x 195 mm; four 60 x 60 mm
• Kitchen sponge
• Water-based glass and ceramic paints: purple, red, dark green
• Paint brush: no. 3 round
• Tracing paper
• Wax pencil, HB pencil
• Mirror, backing board and tile adhesive

Repeat for all the long tiles. Then tape the corner stencil onto a square, sponge, and repeat for all the tiles.

3 Trace the pattern for the swirls for both tiles onto tracing paper. Rub the back of the tracing paper with the wax pencil, and transfer the design onto the tiles (this method allows for better visibility when positioning the pattern on the tiles). Cut the tracing paper the same size as the tile so that the alignment of the swirls will be the same for each tile.

4 Using the round brush and dark green, paint in the swirls. Apply a second coat. Repeat for all the tiles. Allow the tiles to dry for 48 hours, then fire them (see page 11). When cool, mount the mirror and tiles on a board using a strong adhesive.

3 Rub the back of the tracing paper with the wax pencil and transfer the pattern onto the tile.

Bathroom border tiles

Add a personal touch to your bathroom tiles by adding a colourful stencilled design to white ceramic tiles. The tiles are stencilled and then oven-fired to make the paint more durable, before being fixed to the wall.

METHOD

1 Enlarge the pattern (see page 59), checking that it is the correct size for your tiles. Using carbon paper, transfer the pattern onto a piece of cardboard. Cut the cardboard the same size as the tiles.

2 Carefully cut out the pattern with the scalpel and metal ruler. Take care that you do not cut through the connecting 'bridges' on the finer parts of the stencil.

3 Tape the cardboard stencil on the tile. Dip the sponge in the blue paint and dab the excess off onto scrap paper until the sponge leaves a fine, even texture. Sponge over the stencil twice to build up an even colour. Carefully remove the stencil and use it to sponge the remaining tiles, following the same technique. Clean up smudges with damp cotton buds, or allow the paint to dry and scrape off paint errors with a scalpel.

4 Paint in the background using the round brush and yellow paint. Leave a small white gap between the blue pattern and the yellow background. Allow to dry before applying a second coat to any patchy areas.

5 Leave the tiles to dry for 48 hours and then fire them (see page 11).

EQUIPMENT

- Carbon paper
- Pencil
- Cardboard
- Cutting mat
- Scalpel
- Metal ruler
- Masking tape
- White ceramic tiles: 200 x 95 mm
- Fine kitchen sponge
- Water-based glass and ceramic paints: light blue, yellow
- Cotton buds
- Paint brush: round no. 3

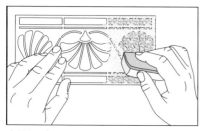

3 Dip the sponge into blue paint, dab off the excess paint and sponge over the surface to build up the colour.

Give an existing tiled wall a touch of colour by adding a border of sunny tiles. Tiles can be stencilled when in position on the wall, but remember that the paint may scratch easily because the tiles will not have been fired.

Etching cream can produce subtle decorative effects in minutes. This glass table top provides a flat, easy surface to work on, but you might like to practise your technique on drinking glasses or even a small mirror.

Etched glass table

The etching technique is easier than you might think. Simply spread the etching cream over a stencil, let the cream do its work, and then wash it off to reveal a subtle, etched design.

METHOD

1 Wash the glass table top with soap and water. Allow the glass to air-dry.

2 Photocopy the wreath from the pattern on page 60 and enlarge it as indicated, or according to the dimensions of your table top.

3 Position the pattern over the self-adhesive vinyl and tape it in place. Using the scalpel, carefully cut out the stencil. As the pattern repeats itself around the table, cut out six (or more, if necessary) stencils.

4 Stick the vinyl stencils around the glass, overlapping each piece. Try to maintain an even amount of spacing between sections. Then smooth the surface down to remove any air bubbles or creases.

EQUIPMENT

- Circular glass table top
- Self-adhesive vinyl
- Masking tape
- Scalpel
- Cutting mat
- Rubber gloves
- Glass etching cream
- Spatula or plastic knife
- Toothpicks
- Kitchen sponge

5 Wearing gloves, stir the etching cream. Then use a spatula to apply a large amount of cream over the exposed areas of the stencil. Spread the cream as if you were icing a cake and pierce any air bubbles.

6 Leave the cream on the glass for about 15 minutes (or according to the manufacturer's directions). After this time, scrape off the excess cream and return it to the container.

7 Rinse the etched surface with water to remove the remaining cream. Use a damp sponge to wipe over the surface (throw away the sponge when finished). Remove the stencil and leave the glass to dry.

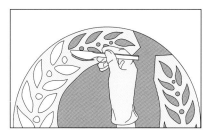

5 Wearing rubber gloves, spread the etching cream over the exposed areas of the stencil.

Name plaque

Create a warm welcome to your home with this pretty name plaque painted on white tiles. All the letters of the alphabet are provided in the template pages, so you can choose any name you want for your house.

METHOD

1 Using the letters provided in the pattern on page 61, trace over the design and appropriate letters to make up the house name. Once you have transferred the design, enlarge (or reduce) the pattern, depending on the size of your tiles. Alternatively, draw the design by hand.

2 Stick the three tiles together by placing masking tape on the back of them. Using carbon paper, transfer the design onto the tiles by carefully tracing around the lettering, roses and leaves. Remove the pattern, carbon paper and masking tape (on the back of the tiles).

3 Working on one tile at a time, paint the letters using a no. 1 brush

EQUIPMENT

• Tracing paper
• Pencil
• Three white tiles: 10 x 10 cm (4 x 4 in)
• Masking tape
• Carbon paper
• Round paint brushes
• Water-based glass and ceramic paints: black, burgundy, dark green
• Cotton buds
• Timber for mounting the tiles and framing, tile adhesive

and two coats of black paint. Allow the paint to dry between coats.

4 Paint the roses using burgundy and the no. 1 brush. Paint the leaves with dark green and a no. 1 round brush. Paint the vines using a no. 00 brush.

5 Leave to dry for at least 24 hours. Place the tiles in a cold oven. Set the oven temperature to 150–160 degrees Celsius and bake for 35 minutes. Turn off the oven and leave the tiles inside until they are cool.

6 Mount the tiles and frame with a timber border.

4 Working on one tile at a time, paint the leaves using dark green. Add in the vines using a fine brush.

44

This dainty rose pattern has been designed to complement the name of the house although it could be used for any house name. Alternatively, a different pattern could be designed to suit your needs.

Livingroom window

A window is the perfect surface for glass painting as the light really intensifies the bright colours. This design is first outlined with outliner paste, and then the segments are filled in with paint. If preferred, you can use liquid leading instead of outliner.

EQUIPMENT

- Masking tape
- Black outliner paste
- Scalpel
- Paint brushes: no 4 flat, no. 2 round
- Glass and ceramic paints: yellow, dark purple, dark green, burgundy
- Palette
- Toothpicks
- Cotton buds

HINT

To speed up the drying time of the paint use a hair dryer, but don't hold the heat too close to the paint or it may scorch.

METHOD

1 Wash the window using warm, soapy water and allow it to air-dry.

2 Enlarge the pattern (located on page 55) to the required size and tape it to the outside of the window. If this is not practical, use a wax pencil and draw the motif directly onto the pane of glass.

3 Holding the tube of outliner paste at a slight angle, gently squeeze the tube to push the paste out through the nozzle. Try to keep the pressure on the tube steady to ensure an even flow of paint. You may need to practise this first on a piece of paper. Replace the cap after use to prevent the paste from hardening and blocking up the fine tip. See the box on page 35 for more information.

4 Using the flat brush, drop small amounts of paint into the top of each segment, following the photograph as a guide. Use the brush to spread the paint out and wipe away any runs. Use a small amount of paint at a time to prevent the paint running down the glass and accumulating at the bottom. Allow the paint to dry, then apply a second light coat. Pop any air bubbles with a toothpick.

5 Clean away smudges with a cotton bud, or scrape off any mistakes with the scalpel (when the paint is dry).

6 Leave the window to dry for several days. As the paints can not be fired in the oven, take care not to use harsh abrasives when cleaning the windows. Be aware too, that steam may affect the paint.

Painting on upright surfaces takes more time than painting on flat surfaces and you'll find that your results aren't as neat. To prevent the paint running down the window apply two or three light coats of paint, rather than one thick layer.

It is much easier to paint detailed designs on a flat surface so, if possible, remove the door from its hinges and lay it on a work table or rest it across the top of two chairs. Leave to dry for several days before re-hanging.

Faux stained-glass door

The pattern for this beautiful door was inspired by Art Nouveau designs. The door was purchased from a second-hand building centre, the glass panels were cleaned up and painted, and the timber was sanded and given a light coat of oil.

EQUIPMENT

- Masking tape
- Stencil plastic or heavy plastic sheet
- Liquid leading
- Wooden door with 2 long glass panels
- Tape measure and ruler
- Scissors and scalpel
- Palette
- Glass and ceramic paints: dark green, burgundy, purple
- Paint brushes: no. 4 flat, no. 2 round
- Toothpicks
- Cotton buds

APPLY THE LEADING

1 Following steps 1–3 on pages 33–4, squeeze out strips of liquid leading onto a sheet of plastic. Allow the strips to air-dry for three days.

2 If possible, lay the door flat on a work table, with the surface to be painted facing up.

3 Measure the glass panels and enlarge the pattern to size (this may involve three separate sheets of A3 paper). Cut the pattern to fit behind one glass panel. Tape it in place.

4 Peel off the leading strips and press them onto the front of the glass using the pattern beneath as a guide. Do not overlap the strips but trim them with a scalpel so that they butt neatly against each other. Fill any gaps and joins with a dab of liquid leading and leave to dry.

PAINTING THE GLASS

5 Using the flat brush, dip the bristles into the paint and drop the paint into each segment, following the photograph as a guide for colour. Drop in an ample amount of paint and spread it out with the brush. Use the smaller round brush to push the paint in the corners.

6 After you have applied the paint to one section, check for air bubbles. Burst these with a toothpick. Clean any smudges with damp cotton buds.

7 Allow the door to dry flat for several days before hanging it. As the glass in this door cannot easily be removed and fired, treat the paint with care. Although the paint will harden without firing, the glass must be kept clean with a light dusting: do not get the paint wet.

Rooster mural

You don't need accomplished skills in folk art to complete this mural for the kitchen because the pattern has an easy colour-by-number system for you to follow. The mural is painted using acrylic paints mixed with glass and tile painting medium, which makes the paint suitable for use on ceramic.

EQUIPMENT

- Sixteen white tiles: 10 x 10 cm (4 x 4 in)
- Masking tape
- Pencil
- Tracing paper
- Carbon paper
- Glass and tile painting medium★
- Round paint brushes: no. 4 & no. 1
- Artists acrylic paints★: ultramarine blue, burgundy, black, pine green, brown earth, warm white, red, light yellow

- Palette
- Cardboard
- Scalpel or scissors
- Cutting mat
- Sea sponge
- Low-tack tape
- Cotton buds
- Board for mounting the tiles
- Tile adhesive

★ If preferred, substitute acrylic paints and glass and tile painting medium for water-based glass and ceramic paints.

PREPARATION

1 Using masking tape, stick down the sixteen tiles onto an old board or directly onto the work table to form a large square made up of four rows of four tiles.

2 Using a photocopier or the grid method, enlarge the patterns for the rooster and the background shape. Enlarge the patterns as indicated, or to fit the size of tiles you are using. The two patterns for this project are on page 62.

3 Using carbon paper, transfer the pattern for the rooster onto the tiles, using the step picture below as a

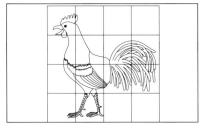

3 Using carbon paper, transfer the pattern for the rooster onto the tiles. Position it on the squares as shown.

You may want to practise painting this rooster on paper before you commit to your tiles. However, even if you do make a mistake, simply wash the paint off the tiles, dry them thoroughly and start again.

guide for positioning the design. Keep a copy of the original pattern nearby as the numbering system will help you later when you are painting the rooster. Set the pattern for the background aside.

PAINTING THE ROOSTER

4 Using the no. 4 brush, paint the tail feathers using ultramarine blue (see the box on the right). You may need to apply two or three coats to achieve a solid coverage, but always allow the first coat to dry before adding the next. Add highlights along the top of some of the feathers using burgundy. Add shading to the bottom part of the feathers using black.

5 Dapple the upper legs and lower body (the areas marked '1' on the pattern) with pine green. To do this, make quick, short brush strokes to give a 'feathery' or dappled effect. Using black, add shading to the underbelly and to the legs.

6 Dapple the lower feathers (the areas marked '2' on the pattern) using black.

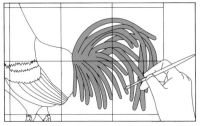

4 Paint the tail feathers in blue. This may take two or three coats to achieve a solid coverage.

PLEASE NOTE

All of the acrylic paints used to complete this project are first mixed with glass and tile medium before use. This makes them suitable for use on ceramics. The medium enables the paint to bond to the ceramic surface and to be fired in the oven.

Generally, the mixture should be in a ratio of 3:1 (3 parts medium to 1 part paint) before use, but check the manufacturer's specific directions. Glass and tile painting mediums generally create a translucent finish, so several coats may be required to create an opaque result, as pictured.

It is recommended that you paint and fire a test tile before firing the complete design.

See the boxes on pages 11 and 31 for further information.

---

7 Working from bottom to top, block in the area marked '3' using two coats of the brown earth acrylic paint. When the paint is dry, use the no. 1 round brush to paint thin, black feathers over the top, working the brush in the same direction.

8 Block in the area marked '4' using a mixture of pine green with a little warm white. Apply the second coat working the brush strokes from top to bottom. When dry, create areas of shadow between the feathers using a little black.

9 Dapple in the breast feathers (marked '5') using burgundy. Apply two coats to achieve a solid coverage. Add in some fine, short 'feathery' strokes using black.

10 Mix red with a very small amount of light yellow and block in the area marked '6'. Add more yellow to this mix and block in the rooster's neck (marked '7' on the pattern). Darken around the edges of these areas using short strokes of brown earth.

11 Paint the rooster's comb and wattle (marked '8') using red and burgundy mixed together in a ratio of 1:1. Apply two coats.

12 Paint the rooster's legs and beak using light yellow with just a little red mixed in. Allow this area to dry and then darken the sides of the legs, the bottoms of the feet and the beak with a little brown earth. Add details to the legs and claws using brown earth acrylic paint and the no. 1 round brush.

13 Add a little light yellow to the brown earth and use this paint to dapple darker feathers on the sides of the neck. Dapple some lighter feathers in the middle of the neck using light yellow with a small amount of brown earth added.

14 Darken the sides of the comb and wattle using ultramarine blue (refer to the photograph above).

Use a finer brush to add in the small strokes of paint around the eye and neck to create a 'feathery' appearance.

15 Using the no. 1 brush, paint the black eye, leaving a thin, white space around the eye and a white area in the centre to suggest a 'reflection'. Darken the area around the eye using small, 'feathery' brush strokes in brown earth.

16 Define the outer feathers of the area '6' using long, continuous brush strokes. Use the no. 1 brush and red to do this.

17 Allow the tiles to dry completely, and then place them in a cold domestic oven. Set the temperature to approximately 165 degrees Celsius and bake the tiles for 30–35 minutes. Turn off the oven and allow the oven to cool completely before removing the tiles.

PAINTING THE BACKGROUND

18 Using carbon paper, transfer the pattern for the background onto a small piece of cardboard. With the scalpel, cut out the shape, including the hole in the middle. Try to do this by rotating the cardboard, so that the cutting movement is more fluid and produces a neater edge.

19 Tape the stencil onto the first blank tile (for this project there are four, but this will depend on the size of your rooster and how you have positioned it on the tiles).

20 Mix up warm white, pine green and brown earth acrylic paints in a ratio of 8:2:1 respectively. Dip the sea sponge into the paint and dab off the excess onto scrap paper. Sponge over the tile stencil, gradually building up the intensity of colour. Repeat this to complete the remaining three blank tiles.

21 As the other tiles are partially obscured by the rooster, you need to create a mask to cover the painted areas. Place some tracing paper over the area of the rooster that protrudes onto the tile and trace around it with a pencil (you may find it easier to remove the tile from the panel and work on these tiles individually).

22 Cut out this shape and use low-adhesive tape to stick the mask in place. Place the stencil for the background over the tile and sponge the area following step 20.

23 Remove the stencil and mask and use a damp cotton bud to wipe off any mistakes. Fill in any gaps with the no. 1 brush.

24 Allow the tiles to dry completely, and oven-fire them following step 17. As this is the second firing for some of the paints, be aware that these colours may darken slightly after their second firing.

25 Using a tile adhesive or mirror adhesive tape mount the tiles on a board. If preferred, you may want to finish the mural by adding a framed timber border around the tiles.

21 Make a mask by putting tracing paper over the area that protrudes onto the tile, then trace around it.

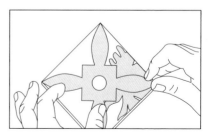

22 Stick the mask in place with low-adhesive tape. Put the stencil for the background over the tile and mask.

Templates

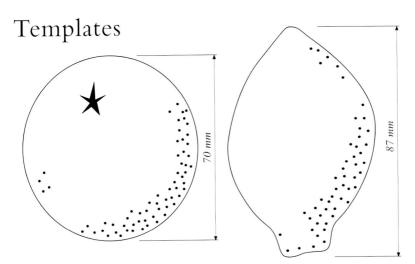

70 mm

87 mm

Citrus bowl (page 22)
Enlarge the images by 140%.

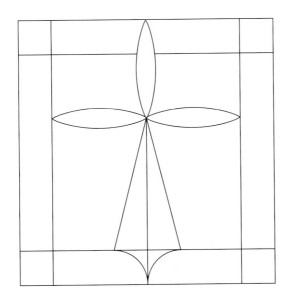

Livingroom window (page 46)
Enlarge the image to suit the size of your window.

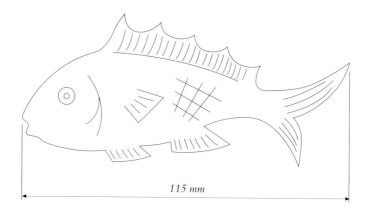

115 mm

Decorative plate (page 16)
Enlarge the image by 128%.

82 mm

Kitchen tiles (page 28)
This pattern is printed at 100%.

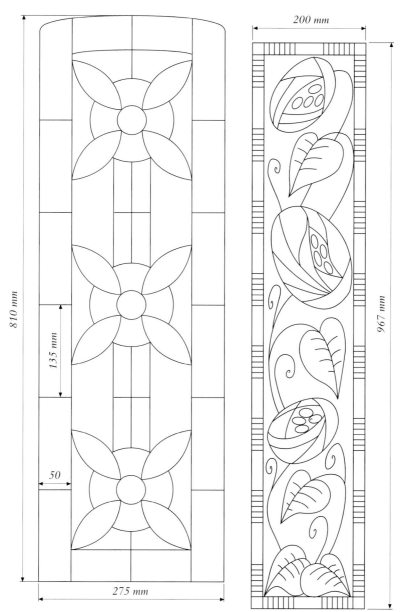

810 mm

135 mm

50

275 mm

200 mm

967 mm

Faux stained-glass cabinet (page 32)
Enlarge the image by 540% (if using a
photocopier enlarge by 200%, then by
200%, and then by 135%).

Faux stained-glass door (page 48)
Enlarge by 645% (on a photocopier enlarge
by 200%, then by 200%, then by 161%).

60 mm

60 mm

60 mm

195 mm

Do not cut out the swirls.

Glasses (page 26)
This pattern is printed at 100%.

Tiled mirror (page 38)
Enlarge the image by 133%.

95 mm

200 mm

Bathroom border tiles (page 40)
Enlarge the image by 138%.

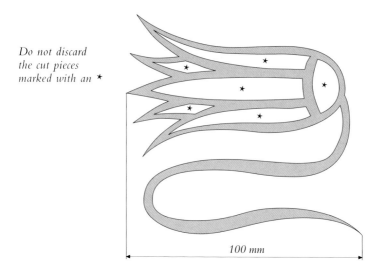

*Do not discard
the cut pieces
marked with an ★*

100 mm

*Lotus flower vase (page 36)
Enlarge the image by 155%.*

450 mm

*Etched glass table (page 42)
Enlarge the image by 600% (if using a photocopier, enlarge by 200%, then by
200%, and then by 150%).*

Rose Cottage

ABCDEFGHI
JKLMNOPQR
STUVWXYZ
abcdefghijklmno
pqrstuvwxyz
1234567890

Name plaque (page 44)
Enlarge the image to suit the size of your plaque.

335 mm

335 mm

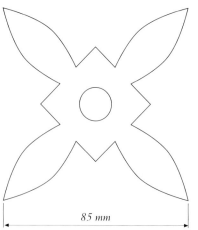

85 mm

Rooster mural (page 50)
Enlarge the pattern for the rooster by
335% (if using a photocopier, enlarge by
200%, and then by 167%).

Background pattern for the rooster mural
Enlarge the pattern by 165%.

Tools for painting glass and ceramic

Some of the most useful tools and materials for painting on glass and ceramic are shown below. Most of the tools can be purchased from your local newsagent or craft store.

MASKING TAPE
Use to mask off straight edges and areas not to be painted

SELF-ADHESIVE DOTS
Available in various sizes; make quick and easy circular masks

SEA SPONGE
Use for sponging paint to achieve a soft, textured effect

COMPASS
Used for drawing accurate circles

COTTON BUDS
Use dry or slightly damp to wipe off paint errors

FINE KITCHEN SPONGE
Gives a finer texture than a sea sponge, and is useful for small or delicate designs

PENCILS
Use 2B or 4B pencils for sketching designs, an H for transferring designs, and a wax pencil to draw directly on to ceramic and glass

SCALPEL
Scissors or a scalpel can be used to cut stencils or masks. A scalpel is better for fine or detailed cutting

PALETTE KNIFE
Small, blunt knife used to spread etching cream

SELF-ADHESIVE VINYL
Removable adhesive used to make stencils or masks. Opaque vinyl is recommended

PAINT BRUSHES
A good range of brushes includes flat, round and fine tips

Index